AF322680

Milk. Anywhere. Everywhere.

Written and Illustrated by Deepthi Kapila
Illustrations created with Adobe Firefly AI image generation
First edition, 2026

ISBN: 979-8-9954687-0-7 (hard cover), 979-8-9954687-1-4 (eBook), 979-8-9954687-2-1 (paperback)
Published by Stillflow LLC United States of America
For permissions contact: stillflow.apps@gmail.com

Dedication

For my kids,
who inspired this book
and eventually grew old enough
for me to actually finish it.

And for every tired mom
feeding their baby somewhere unexpected.

Before We Begin

Breastfeeding can be beautiful, confusing, hilarious, overwhelming — sometimes all before breakfast.

Inside are fifteen real-life moments inspired by nursing positions, seen through the wonderfully chaotic lens of motherhood.

Some might make you laugh. Some might teach you something new. Most will remind you that **you are not the only one figuring this out.**

And if you're in the middle of it right now — **you are doing great.**

Table of Contents

I

Surviving the Early Days

milk. sleepless nights. love.

Midnight Pretzel

Somewhere around 3 a.m. you realize you're twisted into a shape no yoga instructor has ever demonstrated. One arm is numb, the blankets are tangled, and the baby seems perfectly comfortable.

Best for:
Night feeds when sitting up feels like far too much effort.

Helpful reminders:
- Keep baby belly-to-belly with your body
- Bend your knees slightly so you don't roll forward

MOM

The Rocking Chair Trap

You sit down to nurse "for just a minute." Fifty minutes later, you're still there — gently rocking in place — while the baby pauses, reflects deeply on life, and then decides, quite confidently, they might like another round.

Best for:
Cluster-feeding days when the baby keeps coming back.

Helpful reminders:
• Keep baby tummy-to-tummy
• Switch sides if the sucking slows

The Alarm Clock Baby

The sky outside is barely light, but the baby has already declared it morning. You're upright in bed feeding a very alert newborn while the rest of the house sleeps.

Best for:
Early morning feeds when the baby decides the day has started — even if the sun strongly disagrees.

Helpful reminders:
- Support baby's head with your opposite hand
- Bring baby to you instead of leaning forward

The Accidental Nap

You planned to stay awake for this feed. Somewhere between latch and lull, both of you drift off for a few quiet minutes.

Best for:
Those completely exhausted feeds when sleep sneaks up on both of you before the latch is even finished.

Helpful reminders:
• Support baby across your body
• Let your shoulders relax instead of hovering

The Surprise Bite

You're casually feeding your baby when suddenly you get bitten by a tiny shark with brand-new teeth. Apparently this is part of the learning process.

Best for:
Those early teething days when the baby suddenly realizes milk comes with a brand-new set of teeth.

Helpful reminders:
- If baby bites, calmly break the latch
- Offer a teether before trying again

II

Milk in
the Wild

grocery aisles. backseats. anywhere.

The Grocery Aisle Guru

You were halfway through comparing cereal boxes when the baby made an urgent announcement. Suddenly Aisle Seven becomes a perfectly reasonable place for lunch.

Best for:
Quick grocery trips that turn into an unexpected snack break somewhere between produce, coffee and cereal.

Helpful reminders:
- Hold baby upright and close to your body
- Support their neck while they latch

The Backseat Snack Stop

The car is parked, the door is open, and you're sitting in the backseat feeding a baby who absolutely could not wait until you got home.

Best for:
Mid-errand hunger emergencies that refuse to wait politely. Suddenly the back seat is the best restaurant in town.

Helpful reminders:
• Sit beside the car seat or lift baby out briefly
• Turn your whole body toward baby instead of twisting

The Peace Treaty

Your baby gets their vaccine, cries for a moment, and you prepare for chaos. You latch them on and suddenly the peace treaty is signed.

Best for:
Doctor visits when comfort is urgently required. Milk diplomacy works faster than anything in the waiting room.

Helpful reminders:
- Hold baby snug against your chest
- Let them latch quickly for comfort

The Shower Reset

You step into a warm, steamy shower with a tired baby who finally relaxes. It's basically a spa day, minus the quiet and the cucumber water.

Best for:
Sick days or fussy afternoons when you've officially run out of ideas.

Helpful reminders:
- Keep baby upright against your chest
- Maintain secure footing and grip

The Double Lunch

The baby eats. You eat. Ideally both of you finish before the food gets cold and the baby decides the meal is officially finished.

Best for:
When you finally remember that you're also supposed to eat today.

Helpful reminders:
- Rest baby comfortably across your lap
- Support baby's head so one hand stays free

III

Doing It Like a Pro

nailing it. effortlessly.

The One-Handed Chef

You're trying to make dinner, and the baby still needs milk. Somehow you do both at once while stirring the pot and running a surprisingly good football hold.

Best for:

When the baby is hungry and dinner is halfway finished. And both need to happen right now.

Helpful reminders:

- Tuck baby comfortably under your arm
- Keep one hand free for stirring

The Playground Referee

You nurse one. You watch the other climbing something ambitious, ready to yell "Careful up there!" Somehow you still manage a sip of your now-cold coffee.

Best for:
When one child needs milk and another needs supervision. Because apparently everyone needs something right now.

Helpful reminders:
- Cross-cradle gives extra support when sitting on a bench
- One hand can still hold a coffee or point dramatically

The Laptop Latch

You keep the meeting going, and keep the keyboard clicking, while the baby happily snacks through it all. Apparently this is multitasking now.

Best for:
When work calls but the baby does too. One meeting has an agenda. The other has priorities.

Helpful reminders:
• Support baby across your lap so both hands stay free
• Muting the microphone is always wise

Milk.
Anywhere.
Everywhere

The Book Club Feed

You sip warm coffee, nurse the baby, and join the conversation while everyone discusses the book they may or may not have actually read.

Best for:
When you you urgently need a conversation that includes complete sentences.

Helpful reminders:
- Support baby comfortably across your lap
- Armrests and pillows make long chats easier

The Trail Snack

You walk the trail with the baby riding in the carrier until hunger strikes. A quick adjustment, and the adventure continues. These days, snack time fits right into the journey.

Best for:
Walks, hikes, or outdoor exploring with a hungry passenger. Feeding happens while you enjoy the fresh air and sunshine.

Helpful reminders:
- Slide baby into a comfortable nursing position in the carrier
- Keep walking — or pause for a moment — you do you.

you are doing great

Before You Go

If some of these moments felt familiar, that's because
breastfeeding rarely happens in perfect, quiet settings.
It happens in the middle of the night, in grocery store aisles, on
park benches, and sometimes while trying to eat your own lunch.

Wherever you find yourself feeding your baby — **you're doing
great.** And you're not the only one figuring it out.

If you ever want a little extra support, help is closer than you
think — your doctor, obstetrician, pediatrician, a lactation
consultant, or simply another mom who's been there.

Some helpful places to start:
La Leche League International · ILCA · KellyMom

You've got this. And when you need it, help is always there.

www.ingramcontent.com/pod-product-compliance
Lightning Source LLC
Chambersburg PA
CBHW040505160726

48196CB00088B/678